Vocational Bu

6

Business Planning

Keith Brumfitt, Stephen Barnes, Liz Norris & Jane Jones

Series Editor: Keith Brumfitt

Published in 2001 by:
Nelson Thornes Ltd
Delta Place
27 Bath Road
CHELTENHAM
GL53 7TH
United Kingdom

01 02 03 04 05 / 10 9 8 7 6 5 4 3 2 1

A catalogue record for this book is available from the British Library

ISBN 0 7487 6364 3

Illustrations by Oxford Designers and Illustrators

Page make-up and illustrations by GreenGate Publishing Services, Tonbridge, Kent

Printed and bound in Italy by Stige

Contents

Introduction to Vocational Business series

This textbook is one of a series of six covering the core areas of business studies. Each book focuses on vocational aspects of business, rather than theoretical models allowing the reader to understand how businesses operate. To complement this vocational focus, each book contains a range of case studies illustrating how businesses respond to internal and external changes.

The textbooks are designed to support students taking a range of business courses. While each is free standing, containing the essential knowledge required by the various syllabuses and course requirements, together they provide a comprehensive coverage of the issues facing both large and small businesses in today's competitive environment.

Titles in the series

Book 1   **Business at Work**
Book 2   **The Competitive Business Environment**
Book 3   **Marketing**
Book 4   **Human Resources**
Book 5   **Finance**
Book 6   **Business Planning**

Acknowledgements

The authors and publishers would like to thank the following people and organisations for permission to reproduce photographs and other material:
Arla Foods; the Associated Newspapers Group; the British Standards Institute; Guardian Newspapers Ltd; Green & Black's; HMSO; Procter and Gamble Ltd; Radio Times; Selclene Ltd; Worldwide Fruit; Zena Holloway; Corel; Photodisc.

Every effort has been made to contact copright holders, and we apologise if any have been overlooked.

Business Planning

Introduction

This book gives you the opportunity to undertake a feasibility study in which you will establish whether there is a market for your product or service and the costs of development. You will develop a business plan based on the resources needed to make the business a success and how you will run your business and the product or service that it offers.

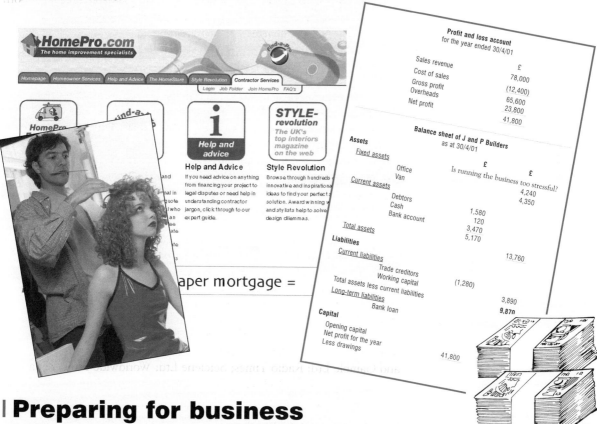

Preparing for business

What will you produce?

Deciding you would like to be self-employed is one thing, deciding what sort of business to run is another. Wanting to work for yourself is not enough. You have to find something to do; something that is profitable or at least earns you enough to live on. The business is unlikely to be a success without a clear idea of what to produce or supply to a market.

Any business venture needs to be carefully planned

1

CASE STUDY

Little Dippers 1

Figure 6.1 *Getting wet (Reproduced by permission of Zena Holloway)*

In 1992 Lauren Heston decided to start her own business. She wanted to make use of her training as a diver, and so her idea was to provide water safety courses for very young babies. The plan involved hiring a local swimming pool for mothers and babies (from six weeks old to one year old) to learn the basics of water safety. Lauren would organise and teach a five-week course, using her own experience of teaching her son. The business started in Sussex with three mothers and their babies attending the first course. The home-based business built up slowly and after 30 months Lauren was able to hire a self-employed part-time teacher to assist. By 2001 over 500 babies a week were taking courses in Sussex, Kent, London and Oxford.

CASE STUDY

Cybercafé

There are now many cybercafés in towns and cities across the UK. The first to open, in 1994, was Cyberia in London. The idea behind this new business was to use the Internet as part of a social event. The risks of opening a completely new venture are always high, as it is difficult to estimate the demand for a new service. Before Cyberia opened, the only other on-line cafés were on the West Coast of America.

Is there a gap in the market?

In the two case studies, both businesses took advantage of a gap in the market. These two new ideas, both in expanding markets, had great potential for future development and expansion. The advantages of being the first, or one of the first, to see a business opportunity are obvious:

- free publicity
- the chance to franchise the concept and name to other entrepreneurs
- opportunities for profit
- chance to develop brand loyalty
- the development of distinctive features.

Unfortunately not every new business has such a clear advantage in its market. In each of the above case studies the business had identified its customers and the segment of the market where it could be successful. A customer profile for each business allowed both Little Dippers and Cyberia to target their marketing effort.

Table 6.1 *Market segment*

Business	Typical customer age	Gender	Income
Little Dippers	25–35	Female	Middle
Cyberia	16–35	Mixed	All groups

By knowing the likely customers and the product or service that can be provided, businesses are in a better position to succeed. One approach to identifying customers for small businesses is to divide the potential market into different segments. The business can then identify a group of potential customers who could create a niche market for the business. There are many factors that could unite potential customers:

- family circumstances such as age, marital status or number of children
- lifestyle choices such as customers who are interested in high-status products
- price such as in the case of customers who always buy the cheapest products
- the home addresses of customers, either in the same area or the same type of property.

Once the potential customers have been identified, through market segmentation, the business is in a better position to consider its market research. Market research does not have to be expensive since there are a number of cheap and reliable ways of finding out who might be a potential customer:

- Family and friends may provide valuable opinions about the business. This approach also has the advantage of publicising your service at the same time.

- Local Business Link, Training and Enterprise Council (TEC), Enterprise Agency, Chamber of Commerce, local Federation of Businesses or Industries can all provide information on local and national market trends.
- The local public (or university) library is valuable for:
  i)   trade journals
  ii) specialist trade directories and databases
  iii) published market research reports such as Mintel Market Intelligence, Euromonitor, Jordans, etc
  iv) government publications such as Business Monitor, Regional Trends and Social Trends
  v)   access to the worldwide web.

There are more expensive ways of researching the market, but these are usually beyond the finances of new businesses. In designing the research for a new business, the entrepreneur begins to advertise the product. Asking people whether they would be interested in buying something is an effective, though expensive, type of promotion. This can lead to a demand for the product when it is launched.

What would your customers want?

It is not enough to just start up in business and hope that customers will find you. Businesses have to sell their products. This can be through advertising and promotion, but it is assisted by knowing why potential customers buy your products. If you understand why consumers buy the products or services, the business can ensure that its advertising and marketing are more effective. Some of the usual factors that influence customers' decisions on what to buy are:

- Appearance – customers often want a particular colour or style to match other products that they already own. For example, Hotpoint and many other companies sell washing machines that are not white. Customers may want a product that looks good – though this is often a subjective opinion. If a business produces something that is just functional, it may not be appropriate for the market. This is particularly the case with clothes as most customers want something that is fashionable, i.e. something that meets their needs and not just something to keep them warm.
- Performance – customers may want a product that is fast, quiet, or economical. Knowing which features are important allows the business to design, make and sell something the market wants.
- Quality – for some customers quality is of paramount importance.
- Reliability – if this is important to customers, businesses will have to ensure that their goods meet the customers' needs.
- Value for money – customers compare what the product is worth to them with the price. If it is seen as good value then consumers will buy the product.

By understanding why consumers buy products, the owner of a business can both create products that are wanted and design advertising campaigns that address the features that customers think are important.

ACTIVITY

What do you want?

The following well known products and services have been sold in Britain for a long time.

Task 1

Work out what you would want from each of these. Your answers should explain why you would buy each of them (even if you do not actually buy any).

Table 6.2 Success in the UK

Product	Important feature 1	Important feature 2	Important feature 3
Apple Macintosh computer			
Sunday Times newspaper			
Armani clothes			
Kit Kat chocolate			

Task 2

Consider the advertisements for two of these products. Do they emphasise the features that you have recorded as important? If they do, it probably means that you fit the company's profile of the typical purchaser of these items. If the advertisements do not appeal to you, in terms of the features that you think are important, you are probably not a typical customer for this product and it is unlikely that you buy the product.

Another way of looking at the reasons why people buy products and services is to consider the demand curve. The following factors influence the demand for a product and these are just as important for a new business as an established firm:

- the price of the product
- the price of the competitors' products
- consumer tastes or preferences
- the income level of the consumers
- the availability of credit
- consumer confidence.

New businesses need to consider the important features associated with their products as well as the demand from consumers. For most small businesses the wishes of the customers are paramount and they effectively determine the success of the business.

 Demand, page 26

> **Note!**
>
> Of all the factors that affect demand, the most important is the price of the product.

CASE STUDY

Little Dippers 2

Figure 6.2 Splashing around (Reproduced by permission of Zena Holloway)

Lauren Heston's water safety business expanded partly because it was popular with parents but also because she could offer what her customers wanted. Initially Lauren offered one five-week course for beginners but it soon became obvious that parents wanted follow-on courses. Through developing new programmes at different levels, Lauren is able to train babies until they are three years old. This allows her to benefit from repeat business, thereby creating loyal customers and saving on the cost of advertising.

Who are your competitors?

If you have a good idea for a new business, the chances are that someone else is trying to run something similar. It is very unusual for businesses, like Cyberia, to enter a market where there are no competitors. Even when you think you are the first to offer a particular service, some market research may well show the presence of existing businesses. You can find out about the competition and the products or services they offer from a variety of sources:

- local trade associations and the Local Authority Economic Development Unit can provide details of the local competitors with statistics on their performance
- local trade directories (available from local trade associations and public libraries), the Yellow Pages and Thompson Directories
- local newspapers and notice boards in community centres, supermarkets, newsagents, etc can be used to identify the competition

- walking round the local area may reveal potential competitors, the location and style of their premises, window displays and price lists where appropriate
- talking to people engaged in businesses similar to the one you are interested in
- asking friends, relatives and potential customers if they can think of other competitors that you do not know about
- attending trade fairs and exhibitions to see what competitors are offering, how they promote their products and trying to obtain their leaflets, brochures and price lists for comparison.

> Searching the worldwide web for your competitors might be profitable but only if you use a suitable search engine, such as Yahoo, Altavista, etc.

What's new?

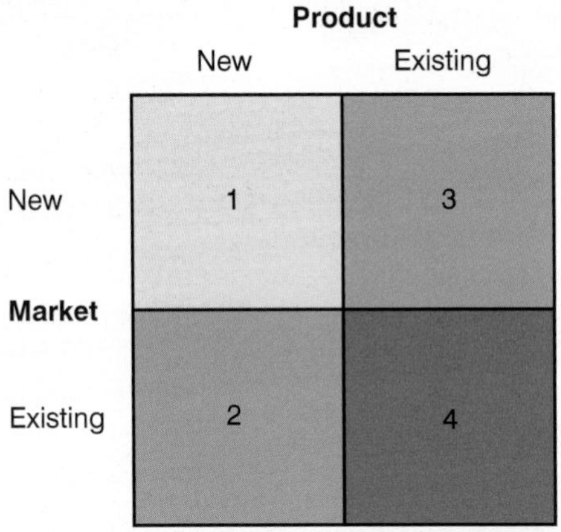

Figure 6.3 *What's new?*

Starting a new business does not mean that everything has to be new. One way of looking at the potential difficulties facing new businesses is to consider exactly what is new. There are four types of new business which can be organised according to a product/market matrix. The matrix allows the owners of the business to examine which aspects of their business are new.

New product in a new market
This is a very high risk strategy as there are few examples of successful businesses to follow. Some of the recent successes are satellite broadcasting, e-commerce and CD-ROM production.

Want to know more?

Electronic commerce, or e-commerce, is straightforward. Other new businesses include p-commerce which makes use of palm-top computer technology, m-commerce which uses mobile phone technology, v-commerce which is video-enhanced e-commerce and d-commerce which uses digital technology.

CASE STUDY

Pringles

Figure 6.4 Reinventing the well known

Not all crisps are the same. Pringles are different. Their packaging, shape and image are all different from other similar products. The introduction of Pringles created a new product in a new market. This ability to create the market allows a new business to be very successful if the customers want to buy the product. Something new in a new market that no one wants to buy is a recipe for business disaster.

New product in an existing market

The introduction of mountain bikes or cruelty-free cosmetics are examples of new products trying to compete in existing markets. In both these cases, the businesses have to establish that their product is better and they must counter any criticism from the existing, more established suppliers.

CASE STUDY

Organic chocolate ice-cream

Green & Black's produce organic chocolate. This is a specialist or niche market and this has helped the business to succeed despite charging a higher price than the competitors. One of the ways the company has **diversified** has been to introduce chocolate ice-cream. This takes advantage of three factors:

- the increasing willingness of some customers to pay a high price for luxury ice-cream, such as that produced by Haagen Dazs or Ben and Jerry's
- the reputation of Green & Black's organic chocolate can be transferred to their ice-cream
- customers expect Green & Black's to use good quality ingredients. By understanding the new market as well as the preferences of their existing customers Green & Black's have successfully entered the ice-cream market.

Figure 6.5 *High class chocolate*

Existing product in a new market

This is often the safest way for a new business to start up. The product (or service) is already accepted in the market and is likely to have a good track record. The difficulty is finding another market that is large enough to make an appropriate profit. Examples of this type of business are franchises and retail outlets which set up new branches.

Franchise, page 21

Existing product in an existing market

This type of new business is likely to face very strong competition since it will have limited opportunities to expand. Without a unique selling point (USP) it will be difficult to establish a loyal customer base, particularly if the existing competitors respond aggressively to any new business, e.g. hairdressers, newsagents or printing services.

ACTIVITY

Milk

Not all milk is the same! We are used to seeing full-fat, semi-skimmed and skimmed milk. Some retailers also sell goat's milk and non-milk alternatives. Not only are there different types of milk, customers can have it delivered to their home or buy it in different-sized cartons. Each is a different product, aimed at a different type of consumer. The latest addition to the product category is Arla Foods' Cravendale PurFiltre milk.

Figure 6.6 *It's not all the same (Reproduced by permission of Arla Foods)*

Tasks

Investigate the price of Cravendale PurFiltre milk and compare it with the competitors'. Why are consumers prepared to pay a higher price for this product?

Who wants to be a millionaire?

People make the decision to become self-employed for a variety of reasons. For some people, often because of a change in circumstances at work, self-employment is seen as a second career. For these people, using their previous skills and contacts forms an important part of being successful in the new venture. For other people, the attraction of working for oneself has always been strong. Businesspeople or **entrepreneurs** are often portrayed as strong-minded, independent people who like to take risks. While this is certainly true of some, many self-employed people have different skills and attributes. Understanding why they are setting up as self-employed allows people to ensure they start an appropriate business.

Key term

An **entrepreneur** organises and manages the people, finance and production necessary for the business to flourish. The entrepreneur keeps the business's profits if it is successful.

Ⓐ CTIVITY

Consider the following factors and place them in order.

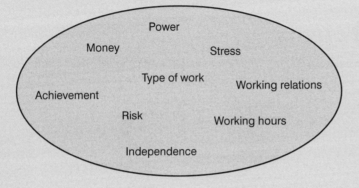

Figure 6.7 *What would you want from a business?*

Ⓐ CTIVITY

Is self-employment for you?

Consider the following ten questions to see whether you seem suited to self-employment.

Yes   No   Maybe

1 Are you self-motivated?
2 Are you sociable?
3 Can you take charge of situations?
4 Can you motivate other people?
5 Are you well organised?
6 Can you make decisions?
7 Are you hard working?
8 Are you trusted by other people?
9 Are you good with money?
10 Do you tend to stick with things once
     you have started?

Figure 6.8 *Self-employment quiz (based on Lloyds TSB's* Starting your own Business*)*

The more times you answered yes to these questions, even a maybe, the more suited you are to becoming self-employed.

One of the disadvantages of being your own boss is the need to have a wide range of expertise. For many people the demands of running their own business are too great since they do not have all the skills and experiences needed to be a success.

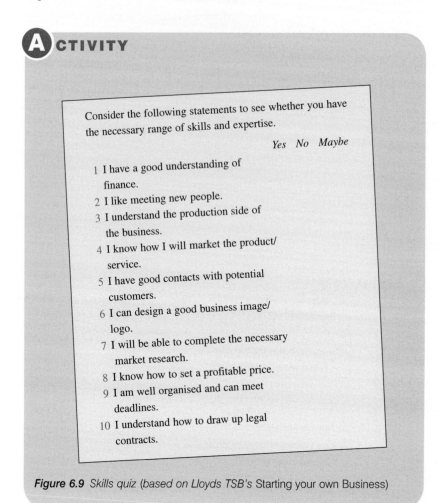

Figure 6.9 *Skills quiz* (based on Lloyds TSB's Starting your own Business)

Many new businesses do not have this full range of expertise and have to employ other people to help with specialised tasks. This is particularly the case with legal and financial matters. Once a business recognises that it cannot provide all the expertise required, new problems of employment are created. Although many new ventures start up as a one-person business, other organisations need staff from the beginning. There are advantages in employing extra staff in any business but there must always be enough money to pay their wages. Taking on extra people is a large responsibility and, in a small business, each extra person has to earn enough income to justify their employment. Deciding whether to employ someone is never easy.

CTIVITY

Ian is a self-employed painter and decorator who is having to turn away jobs because he doesn't have enough time to do all the work. He is considering employing an apprentice to help him with the extra work. What factors do you think he should consider before taking on an assistant?

How could you raise the finance for your business?

 Cash flow, page 47

Raising money can be a time-consuming and difficult part of setting up a new business. Before the business can raise any finance it has to complete its business plan, and work out its cash flow and profit forecast. It is possible that the new business does not need to borrow any money. If finance has to be raised it is important for the business to know:

- how much money is needed
- why the money is required
- when it will be paid back.

Without this basic information, lenders, even if they are family or friends, will not consider making an investment. Once the owners of the business have interested a lender (and this is not always easy), consideration has to be given to the cost of borrowing the money. The interest charged on all borrowed money is referred to as the **annual percentage rate of interest** (APR).

> ## Key term
>
> **APR**, the annual percentage rate of interest, is the standard way of measuring the cost of borrowing money. It is always expressed as a percentage and the higher the figure, the more expensive it is to borrow money.

Internal or external finance

The two main ways of raising finance for a business are from internal or external sources. Each of these sources is likely to be used by any business over its lifetime. The following are common sources of external finance.

External finance
Venture capital

There are many venture capital funds in the UK which invest in new or expanding businesses. Their money is provided by insurance companies, pension funds, individuals and banks. These venture capital fund holders look for successful businesses in need of extra money for expansion and aim to buy shares in these companies. These shares are then sold after a few years, perhaps allowing the fund holders to make a profit on their investment.

Lease

Rather than buying an asset such as premises, some businesses will lease the property. As this is cheaper than buying, it provides savings and therefore access to more funds. This involves two costs:

- the cost of the lease, which is the right to use the premises for a certain period of time, usually a number of years

> External finance is any money raised from outside the business. This can be for a short period of time or for the long term:
>
> - venture capital
> - lease
> - hire purchase
> - fixed term loan
> - overdraft
> - factoring
> - grants
> - trade credit
> - mortgages
> - credit cards.

13

- the monthly or yearly rental on the lease.

Although the business does not own the asset, it is a cheaper and more flexible way of starting a business. If the business does not succeed, the lease can be sold to someone else.

Hire purchase

Businesses, like individuals, buy goods on hire purchase. This allows immediate access to the asset without having to pay the full price. With the hire purchase system the business hires the asset until the final payment is made and then the asset is owned. Although this is an expensive way of buying something, it has the advantage of giving immediate access to the asset.

Fixed term loan

A fixed term loan has to be repaid with interest within an agreed period. It is a cheap way to borrow money and allows the business to plan the repayments. In some cases the loan is secured against a business's assets, which gives the lender the first claim to the asset if the business defaults on repayments.

Overdraft

An overdraft allows a lender to borrow up to an agreed amount of money if needed. This overdraft facility is used when necessary and repaid as soon as possible. This credit facility is often expensive but it does allow a temporary use of additional funds when necessary.

Factoring

Factoring occurs when a business has difficulty collecting the money it is owed from its debtors. These debts are then sold to a factoring agent for about 80 per cent of their value. The factoring agency then collects all the debts. The remaining balance, less the charges, is paid to the business after an agreed period of time. The original business therefore collects most of the money it is owed.

Grants

These funds are the most attractive as they do not have to be repaid. Central government, charities, local government and other organisations will give grants if the business meets certain aims or is located in parts of the country that are eligible for start-up grants.

Trade credit

Whenever a business makes many small purchases it is easier to have an account with the supplier than for different employees to write cheques for each transaction. This is certainly the case when there are a large number of individuals buying supplies from the same source. Privately owned garages, plumbers' merchants, etc often run such accounts for local businesses. These accounts do not need to be settled until the end of the month, or later, and this allows the purchaser to use the month's credit as a source of income besides providing the possibility of a discount because of the volume of trade.

Mortgages
A business can use a fixed asset, such as premises, as security in raising money from banks, building societies or other lenders. This loan is repaid over a number of years. If the borrower is unable to repay the loan or the interest, the lender has the first claim on selling the security to collect the money that it is owed.

Credit cards
Some organisations use a business credit card for spending. This is particularly the case with business expenses such as petrol, entertainment, travel, etc. Occasionally a business credit card can be used to purchase raw materials or supplies, rather than using a customer account. Credit card companies ask for the account to be settled at the end of each month.

Internal finance
In addition to the above external sources of finance, there are some internal sources of finance. These allow businesses to use their own financial resources rather than having to rely on others.

Improved financial controls
One of the most important means of raising finance is through improved financial control. It entails considering whether money is currently being wasted. Sometimes this is an easy task and wastage is obvious. At other times this involves making staff redundant, reducing unnecessary expenditure or collecting debts more quickly.

Retained profits
A business's profits are used to repay the original investors or for investment. In each year businesses aim to use some of their profits for the future expansion of the business.

Sale of assets
Although this is often a drastic solution to a lack of cash, it is possible to sell some of the business's assets. This is sensible if the business is upgrading equipment and changing its production, but it has to be considered carefully because once the assets are sold it will be more expensive to replace them.

Which source of finance should you use?
Once all the potential sources of finance are identified, the entrepreneur has to select which ones are the most appropriate for the business. There are no instant answers as different businesses need different solutions. In deciding how to finance the business, you should consider both the

> **Internal finance is any money raised from within the business. This source is rarely available for starting a new business but it can provide important funds in subsequent years. Internal sources of finance can be:**
>
> - **improved financial controls**
> - **retained profits**
> - **sale of assets.**

initial requirements and the on-going needs. To help you decide, consider the following:

- Is it short-term or long-term finance that is needed?
- How much does each source of finance cost?
- Is collateral or security needed for some sources of finance?
- Will you have to give up part ownership of the business to raise the finance?
- Can the business afford to take risks with its finance?

The answers to these questions will direct the owners of the business towards the right solutions for them. Money for starting a business is not the only reason for raising funds – most people need financial help to keep themselves going until their business generates income. Entrepreneurs are therefore often trying to raise money for:

- capital, which is the one-off expense of starting the business
- working capital to continue trading until the business earns enough income.

The financing of the business can be split into two separate stages: funds to start the business, and additional funds once the business is trading. At both stages finance can be raised from sources outside the business or from the business and its owner's internal sources. All businesses have to make use of both internal and external sources of finance, so it is mainly a question of getting the right balance. Although there is a wide range of sources of income available to new businesses, each one has its advantages and its costs.

A CTIVITY

Little Dippers

We have already looked at Lauren Heston's business and how she started from home in 1992. Initially the water safety training courses did not need large amounts of initial capital, but as the business expanded it needed access to further funds for use as working capital.

Task 1
Why would Lauren have needed start-up finance for her business?

Task 2
Why does Lauren need large amounts of working capital?

Task 3
Which sources of finance would you recommend for Lauren to meet her current and future needs?

Taking out insurance

All businesses need to have insurance to protect themselves from legal action and accidental damage. Other risks include theft, public liability, fire, etc and protection can be provided by an insurance firm. Each type of protection is assessed separately and the premiums depend on the amount of insurance required, the location of the business, the nature of the business's work, the size of the business and any previous claims.

Is it legal?

Having decided to start a business, there are various important legal issues to consider. Parliament and the European and British courts place a number of obligations on businesses that have to be met. These include:

- employment issues
- contractual rights and responsibilities
- licensing requirements
- public sector liability
- the need for insurance.

Each of these will need to be considered before a business can begin to trade. Most everyday business activities take place within a legal environment. For example, insurance against accidents, buying goods and services and employing staff are all legally binding contracts.

Want to know more?

There are many different licensing organisations in the UK, each of which considers whether the owners are allowed to operate their business. Although it is not possible to give a full list of which agency you need to apply to, some of the main agencies are as follows.

Table 6.3 Licences

Business	Agency
Child minding, private car hire, night-clubs, pet shops, residential care, street trading	Local Authority Licensing Department
Waste management, abstraction of water, scrap metal processing	Environmental Agency for England and Wales
Hotels, restaurants, hairdressers	Local Authority Environmental Health Department
Heavy goods vehicles or bus services	Vehicle Inspection Executive Agency
Sale of alcohol in any venue	Magistrates
Any business involving lending money	Office of Fair Trading

Are you ready to start?

Before starting a new business venture, it is important to check you have planned as much as possible. There will always be some surprises for a new business but the more you predict before you start the better. The following twelve questions will help you decide whether you are ready to start a new business.

ACTIVITY

Ready, Steady, Go!

Consider the following twelve questions to see whether you are ready to start your business.

Yes   No   Maybe

1 Have you defined your idea/product/service?
2 Is your market research complete?
3 Do you know who you will sell to?
4 Is the market large enough to make a profit?
5 Does your product meet the needs of your market?
6 Do you know if your product differs from the products of competitors?
7 Have you talked to potential customers?
8 Have you decided on a price for the product?
9 Will your market grow in the future?
10 Do you know who will make the product?
11 Do you know the costs of setting up?
12 Are you aware of the risks involved?

Figure 6.10 Ready, Steady, Go! (based on Lloyds TSB's Starting your own Business)

| Starting up

Once you have decided you are ready to establish a new business, there are further considerations. A new business needs to consider all the different areas of operation and will require:

- a marketing strategy
- an operations plan
- a human resources plan

- a financial plan
- statements of operational principles.

These requirements form a framework for the well planned business and guide entrepreneurs through the initial phases of running their own business.

Taking aim

There are risks in setting up a business – things may not always go well and the business might collapse. The better the business is planned the more you can reduce the risks. To help you plan the business you should consider the following:

- What type of business should you set up?
- What are the aims of your business?
- Should you work alone?

Before starting a business, it is important to know what can be achieved. The objectives of a business can be expressed as specific targets or goals, which will form the focus of the business's activity. These business goals can be written as a mission statement which explains the purpose of the business. The mission statement provides a clear focus to activities and can be used to check that the business is moving in the right direction.

What type of business?

Deciding what type of business to organise and run is a key decision. Most self-employed people work within the service sector but there are other opportunities. Sometimes people forget that there are openings in manufacturing and construction for new businesses, particularly when the economy is expanding.

Want to know more?

In 2001 there were over three million self-employed people in the UK. There has been a growing trend in self-employment over the past ten years as businesses reduce the number of people they employ, the government encourages self-reliance and the labour market becomes more flexible.

Table 6.4 Self-employment in the UK (Source: Social Trends)

Region	Agriculture and fishing	Manufacturing	Construction	Services	Total self-employed
England	6.3%	7.9%	24.5%	61.3%	2,820,000
N. Ireland	27.4%	n/a	25.5%	42.7%	81,000
Scotland	12.0%	5.9%	19.8%	62.3%	225,000
Wales	16.7%	7.1%	24.8%	51.3%	16,000

Although the service industries have the greatest number of self-employed, there are many entrepreneurs in all sectors of the economy.

Another early decision for new businesses is which type of legal structure to use. Whatever is decided is not necessarily final because it is always possible to change the business structure, though this is expensive. New businesses can select from one of the following structures:

Figure 6.11 Business structure

If the new business involves only one person, the choice is between being a sole trader or a limited company. If two or more people wish to work together, the choice is between a partnership, limited company or a co-operative. Each type of business structure has its own advantages and the decision of which structure to adopt is often personal.

There are a number of factors that should be considered before the decision about which type of business structure to use is made. These factors include consideration of:

- your personal liability for debts
- whether it is easy to prepare the financial accounts
- the ability to borrow money
- the tax position.

Should you work alone?

Multinational companies often work together, sharing marketing and production costs and promoting each other's business. Small businesses can also pool resources and expertise to save money and provide a better service.

ⒸASE STUDY

Austrian and Swiss airlines

Airline operators are typical of large businesses attracted by the advantages of collaboration. Three airline operators jointly promote all the internal flights in Austria and Switzerland. Even though Austrian Airlines, Tyrolean Airlines and Swissair are multi-million pound businesses, they are small by airline standards. Together they are able to provide a better service to their customers.

Working with others can include setting up a partnership or co-operative, employing someone to work for you or working collaboratively with another business. Each of these options allows the new business to gain access to extra expertise and experience, though each has its disadvantages. In a partnership or co-operative there is a genuine sharing of tasks to the benefit of all involved. For the sole trader an employee receives a wage in return for completing certain duties. Employees do not share the risks or the rewards of the business as they will be paid regardless of the success of the sole trader.

When businesses work together, as with the airlines, the costs are reduced through the sharing of information, marketing, research spending or staff. Deciding whether to go it alone or share the risks and rewards is an important decision in the setting up of a business.

Setting up a franchise

When people first become self-employed they do not always start up a new business. There are two other approaches to self-employment:

- taking over an existing business
- taking up a franchise.

Key term

A **franchise** involves two businesses. The original business (the franchisor) gives the other business (the franchisee) the right to sell or produce its goods and services in return for payment.

Want to know more?

Table 6.5 Starting a business

How to start a business	Advantages	Disadvantages
Buy an existing business	Established reputation Existing customers Experienced staff Physical facilities in place	Staff and customers may not be happy with new owner May be run-down facilities Location may not be good
Set up a new business	Free to decide everything Create your own image/style Locate where you want	Hard to establish reputation No customers Hard to raise funds A lot will need to be done
Start up a franchise	Training is provided Finance can be easier to raise Established reputation Others have succeeded On-going help	Restricted control Cost of buying franchise Image is controlled by franchise owner

A franchise is a contractual licence granted by one business (or individual) to another. This

- allows the franchisee to carry on a particular business
- allows the franchisor to have some control over the franchisee
- requires the franchisor to provide assistance and help
- requires the franchisee to pay for these rights.

CASE STUDY

Kall Kwik

An increasingly popular way for people to set up a new business is by means of a franchise. In 1996 over 40 per cent of all retail sales in the USA were through franchised outlets. Kall Kwik is just one of the many organisations that allows entrepreneurs to set up their own business. Kall Kwik's success is based on:

- a tried and tested system
- a valuable brand name
- corporate support and back-up
- a high chance of business success.

This winning combination has encouraged many people to start their own printing and copying business. Working with an established business identity reduces the risks of being in business but there are often substantial set-up costs to be paid to the franchisor as well as an ongoing financial arrangement.

A marketing strategy

The four elements of the marketing mix (price, product, place and promotion) exist for new businesses and it is important to get this right. Each of the four elements of the mix should convey the same message. For example, if the business wants an upmarket, high value, exclusive image then the marketing mix should reflect this by:

- setting a high price
- using expensive packaging
- advertising in exclusive magazines
- only selling the product in expensive shops.

It is only when the four elements of the mix are consistent that the business can expect to be successful.

Getting the marketing mix right

CASE STUDY

Gusto

The original Gusto drink, launched in 1990, started the demand for energising non-alcoholic drinks. Gusto now produces a range of uplifting herbal drinks. In designing the product, considerable care has been taken over the marketing mix. The product is designed for a particular audience, sells at a reasonable price of £1.59 per bottle and is stocked by a few select retailers and nightclubs. The advertisement demonstrates how the product has been designed for its audience. Marketing expressions such as 'Do it with Gusto' and 'It's the surreal thing' aim to appeal to potential customers.

In this example the four P's of marketing can be seen working together. The market for the drink is likely to be teenagers and twenty-somethings with a particular lifestyle. A similar approach to co-ordinating the marketing can be seen on the launch of the company's latest product, Gusto Goddess. The company describes the drink in the following terms: 'Gusto Goddess, lightly sweetened with apple juice, in place of sugar, offers women optimum quantities of all these natural health-boosters. But men can enjoy Gusto Goddess too, without any qualms – it simply brings the yin into balance with the yang, maximising energy function.' This is all part of the marketing, and the advertising copy is written to appeal to the company's potential customers. References to yin and yang, sugar-free and health are all included to meet the perceived wishes of a young, health-conscious clientele.

Figure 6.12 *The Love Bomb*

ACTIVITY

Selclene

Figure 6.13 Hired help

With an increasing number of people employing cleaners, a new franchise has been set up to provide a domestic cleaning service. Selclene holds a database of available cleaners and charges them to householders at an hourly rate. Selclene's service includes insurance and the screening, selection and vetting of cleaners. This removes any uncertainty from employing a cleaner.

Task

Selclene has designed its marketing to appeal to a particular market segment. How would you describe this market segment? Do you think this is a successful marketing strategy for the franchise?

Setting the price

The first requirement in the marketing mix is the product. Deciding on what product or service to sell influences the other decisions on the four P's of marketing. The second stage of the marketing mix entails setting the price. The business must know who its potential customers are and be aware of the competition, before setting the price for its products. If the price is too high the business will not sell enough, but if it is too low the business will not make a profit. A step-by-step approach is needed which combines considering the competition, the market and the product. The following seven-step approach allows you to be sure your price is right in your market.

⇨ STEP 1

What position does the product have in the market? Try to establish how potential customers see the product – is it new, reliable, innovative, stylish? When a business knows how the product (or service) is viewed by customers, it understands better what they are prepared to pay.

⇨ STEP 2

Can the product's image be improved? Can the product or service be changed to make it more valued by customers? A different product (or service) will have a different position in the market and therefore a different price.

⇨ STEP 3

What is the competition like? By considering rivals' products (or services) a business will understand whether its products should be more cheaply or more expensively priced than those of its competitors.

⇨ STEP 4

What will the strategy be? This step involves deciding the general approach to pricing – whether the business wishes to set the same prices as, or higher or lower prices than, those set by the competition.

⇨ STEP 5

What should the price range be? The business tries to establish a range of possible prices and for each price it works out the profit based on the business's costs and predicted sales.

⇨ STEP 6

What is the best price for the business? This step entails selecting the actual price.

⇨ STEP 7

Can the price be tested? The business tries to test this price with some of its customers. Sometimes this price could be used for the first three months of business or in one section of a market. It can then be reviewed in the light of customers' responses.

Figure 6.14 *Setting the price*

Ⓒ ASE STUDY

CD prices

Price is not the only factor that matters for customers. Although price is a very important ingredient in the success of the business, consumers do not always buy the cheapest product. The above data shows that the price of CDs varies. It is interesting to ask, 'Why don't consumers buy the cheapest product?' Price, as one aspect of the marketing mix, is an important element in determining the business's success but it is not the only element. You may wish to consider why you do not always buy the cheapest CD available.

Figure 6.15 How the prices of compact discs compare (Source: Metro, 19 November 1999)

Artist & Album	Our Price	WH Smith	Tower Records	Boots (from 26 Nov)	Amazon (UK website)	Amazon (US website)	US Retail
Mel C *Northern Star*	£13.99	£12.99	£13.99	£9.99	£9.99**	£8.00**	£8.63
Geri Halliwell *Schizophonic*	£13.99	£12.99	£13.99	£9.99	£9.99**	£8.63**	£8.63
Gomez *Liquid Skin*	£14.49	£12.99*	£13.99	£9.99	£9.99**	£8.00**	£10.48
Charlatans *Us and Us Only*	£14.49	£12.99*	£13.99	£9.99	£9.99**	£8.63**	£8.63

*Special offer – reduced from £13.99, **Add £1.30 for postage

What is the demand?

Once the price of the product has been decided, a business will have some idea of the demand. A higher price than that set by its competitors will often lead to a lower demand. There are clear links between price and demand. The demand curve was a theoretical model of this relationship, which in practice is very hard to establish.

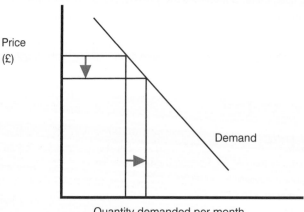

Figure 6.16 What is the demand?

The demand curve above only predicts that if the price rises then the demand will fall. A small business will not be able to estimate actual sales at each price level as this would need a great deal of expensive market research. Small businesses have two main methods of estimating the demand for a product in an existing market:

- identifying the potential customers and adding together their likely purchases; this approach is useful if you expect to sell to a small number of customers.
- estimating how much each of your potential customers spends on your product or service; this is useful if there are a large number of potential customers. For example, a hairdresser may estimate that each female customer, on average, will spend £15 per month on her hair.

Each of these two approaches would give the business some idea of its sales but the techniques only work when there is an established market for a well known product. If your product or service is completely new then other, more expensive market research approaches will be required.

What's in a name?

Once the product and price have been decided, promotion is the next priority. Part of the promotion strategy for a new organisation is deciding on the business's name. Selecting the right name for a business or product is very important. In the above case study, Gusto conveys a message of enthusiasm, activity and newness. The name of the product should be part of the marketing of the product or service and reinforce the image the business is aiming for.

ⒸASE STUDY

Swampy™

Figure 6.17 *Whose name is it?*

The name of Swampy has been registered as a trademark but not by the well known tunnel protester. A Hull businessman has registered the nickname and will be able to use it as part of any marketing activity.

Deciding the name of a business is never straightforward. Some of the considerations include the following.

- ■ **Does the name create the image you are looking for?**

- ■ **Is it easy to pronounce and spell? (to avoid confusion)**

- ■ **What does the name mean in other languages? (if you wish to sell overseas)**

- ■ **Does it help your business stand out from the competitors?**

CTIVITY

Using the knowledge you have of environmental activists, identify how the businessman could make use of this name. For the idea to be a success, you need to identify the four elements of the marketing mix for each idea that you suggest.

There are a number of information sources for anyone trying to decide what name to use for a business.

- • The leaflets 'Business Names – Guidance Notes' and 'Company Names – Guidance Notes' are available from the Department of Trade and Industry's Companies Registration Office.
- • Public libraries and local trade organisations have access to catalogues and databases of existing business names and trademarks (if you are trying to register a name that is the same as a trademark).
- • Companies House, the Trademarks Registry and the Office of Fair Trading will also carry out research of their own indexes and databases.
- • Business Names Registration plc will make sure the name chosen meets the regulations, will send you the documents needed and will put your name on the register to protect you against copying.

Consulting a solicitor may save legal problems later.

Shared promotion

Figure 6.18 Joining forces
(Reproduced by permission of
Worldwide Fruit)

CASE STUDY

New Zealand apples

For small businesses there can be advantages in joining a trade association or group of similar producers; for example apple producers could find it very difficult to promote their own business without the support of a large organisation. Enza used to be the trademark for New Zealand apple growers and formed part of the business's marketing strategy. Trademarks have also been used to promote Cape produce from South Africa.

CASE STUDY

Austrian and Swiss airline chocolate

Earlier we looked at how three airlines worked together to provide a better service for their customers. Austrian Airlines, Tyrolean Airlines and Swissair also undertake joint marketing projects to promote all three businesses. Even the complimentary bar of chocolate given out on internal flights promotes all three airlines. Although the businesses compete with each other for customers leaving Austria and Switzerland, they are happy to collaborate in the domestic section of their market.

New businesses often find the early days very difficult. Building up the business can take a long time and be expensive. Working with established businesses, either through a trade association or through a collaborative agreement, can reduce these difficulties. By drawing upon the established reputation and success of other companies, a new business has a greater chance of success.

Getting the goods to market

In the earlier case studies, different approaches to distributing goods and services have been considered. Getting goods to consumers should not be taken for granted. In many of the case studies consumers collect the goods or services, for example Little Dippers and Cyberia. In others, the manufacturer has to set up a distribution system to supply retailers, for example Gusto drinks. An increasingly important distribution system, as well as a marketing device, is the Internet. Many products or services can be supplied online.

ⒸASE STUDY

Virtual record stores

Figure 6.19 *Many people now look to the Internet to buy music*

The first UK online record trade took place in June 1998. Using touch-screen computer, customers select 20 tracks from the online database. These tracks are then written onto a compact disc. This allows consumers to buy customised CDs, it allows the record companies and artistes more opportunities to sell lesser known tracks, and payment is all completed online. This idea was further developed by musicmaker.com which offers a service through kiosks similar to the existing instant photo booths. Beginning in October 1999, the company had 750,000 tracks available to customers. By selling direct to the public, virtual music companies do not have the expenses of traditional record stores and some analysts in the record industry believe all popular music could be sold and distributed this way in the future.

| Human resource plan

The process of recruitment for large businesses is complicated since it involves a job description, a person specification, designing criteria to select the shortlist of candidates, notifying the people who will be interviewed, the interview process, keeping records of the decisions (in case of appeal or complaint), collecting references and making the offer of employment. Few small businesses will go through this whole process. They will look for shortcuts to save time and money. Employing a friend, a member of the family or someone who is recommended is the more usual way of recruiting staff.

There are four main ways of letting people know you are interested in employing someone:

- **advertisements**
- **using family, friends and business associates**
- **using a recruitment consultancy**
- **recruiting directly from schools, colleges or universities.**

©ASE STUDY

Little Dippers 3

Figure 6.20 *Going overboard (Reproduced by permission of Zena Holloway)*

When Lauren Heston started her water safety business, she taught all the classes, completed her own accounts, answered the telephone enquiries, and booked the swimming pool in addition to the dozens of other things that self-employed people have to do. When the time came to employ other trainers and some administrative staff, it was important to have people whom she could trust. One of the first decisions was whether to employ staff or work with other self-employed people. The other trainers who work with Lauren are all self-employed and take care of their own income tax, pension requirements and holidays. This arrangement reduced Lauren's administrative workload and suited the needs of the trainers.

Individuals cannot just decide to be self-employed or employed. The decision has to be made by the Inland Revenue (Tax Office). In most situations it is obvious whether someone is employed or self-employed but sometimes there can be some doubt. The Inland Revenue decides your employment status by considering the following:

- Who decides where the work takes place?
- Who decides what fee, salary or wage is paid?
- Who decides when the work has to be completed?

Can you manage your own time?

Businesses needing assistance may not wish to employ extra staff immediately. There are other ways of dealing with high workloads. New businesses should think about how they would manage any sudden increase in the workload. Some of the more usual approaches are:

- seeking help from members of the family
- using an employment agency for temporary staff to help meet the extra demand
- employing commission based staff
- using part-time staff who may be enough to meet the extra demand.

It is only when the extra work continues and is likely to be permanent that the business should consider recruitment. No business should take on an extra worker if the extra work is temporary.

What are the costs of employment?

Although it is always helpful to employ another person, the small business has to consider whether it is profitable. There are obvious expenses in taking on an employee, such as the salary or wages, National Insurance contributions, possible overtime or commission and any other benefits. There are often other costs that are not so obvious such as:

- sick pay when the employee is ill
- additional insurance costs
- a pension contribution (sometimes paid by employer)

- use of a vehicle, desk, space in an office, telephone, heating, etc
- extra equipment such as another computer, telephone, etc.

All these costs have to be covered by the employer. It is therefore very important to be certain that the new employee will make a large enough contribution to cover all these extra costs. In some circumstance it is cheaper to improve the efficiency of those already working in the business, for example by investing in new technology or staff training.

Training courses

One of the key ways to improve the efficiency or competence of the existing staff is to use training courses. These are provided at the local college, university, local government training centre or private centre. Training exists for the owner of the business as well as the employees and will cover all aspects of running a business. The Business Links network offers a range of courses that could be of value for small businesses.

Training does not have to be provided by outside organisations; many businesses run their own training for new and existing staff. It may also be possible for small businesses to take advantage of training provided by other employers if there are good business links. Other sources of training can be via a trade association or through a freelance trainer or consultant.

Training should always be considered before employing an extra worker. It is both a cheaper and more effective way of motivating existing staff. Employing someone can give misleading messages to the existing staff about their competence and the amount of work that is expected.

| Operations plan

The business's operations plan will consider how the products or services are to be produced and how the quality will be monitored. This will entail establishing who will supply the business with raw materials, where the product will be made, what use will be made of technology and how the suppliers can maintain delivery schedules.

Can you organise production?

One of the first decisions regarding production is where to locate the business. Many new businesses are set up near where the owner lives. Traditionally there were seven factors to consider in deciding the location of any enterprise, though each of them varied in importance according to the type of business:

- nearness to the market
- nearness to raw materials
- the influence of the climate
- the importance of transport costs

> **Many people at work get inundated with bits of paper but there are four actions to help you deal with letters, memos and circulars:**
>
> - **throw them away**
> - **put them in the right files**
> - **pass them to someone else**
> - **respond to them.**

> **Note!**
>
> One of the advantages of working with a small group of suppliers can be the shared responsibility to improve quality through a better trained workforce.

- nearness of suppliers
- available skilled labour
- cost of land and premises.

Modern businesses do not consider all these factors. Each new business will consider some of the factors, as each has different priorities. For example, e-commerce depends on an efficient and reliable distribution system; call centres and telephone banking seek to minimise their costs; and many sole traders decide to work from home because of the convenience.

What should the level of output be?

Whether a business is manufacturing or selling services, it is important that the level of output should closely match sales. We need to think of the business as market-led. This means that output is driven by sales rather than the other way round. It is useful to think of each sale 'pulling' output through the series of processes that make up the business enterprise. The reverse image of output 'pushing' sales is risky and inefficient.

What happens when output and sales move out of line?

If output is too high, then unsold products will accumulate as stock. This is costly to store and insure, but most importantly it ties up financial resources that are earning nothing. If output is too low, then customers will experience frustration and delays when products are out of stock. The reputation of the business will suffer and some customers will be lost to the competition.

Unfortunately it is not always easy to ensure that output and sales closely match. For a market-led business there are several key factors that make success more likely:

- thorough market research that allows reasonable accuracy in predicting the pattern of sales
- analysis of recent sales data to improve sales forecasting – this is likely to be cheaper and more effective with the use of IT
- supply chains that are shorter and carry faster communications – this means that unexpected increases or decreases in demand can quickly be transmitted backwards through the processes of the business and to its suppliers
- flexibility in production where output can change focus between product types.

It helps if the ratio between fixed costs and variable costs is not too high and the business can carry a small amount of spare capacity (say 10 per cent). This means that the level of output can be changed relatively quickly and without too much additional cost. In practice, sales of any product will vary – apparently at random – from period to period. These 'sawtooth' variations are usually met from stock or through small rises and falls in output. Having some spare capacity is particularly valuable when there is a major surge in sales. This often occurs in a cyclical or

Market research, page 3

seasonal pattern – for example, as demand increases before Christmas. No business can ever achieve exactly the right output of its products. But every enterprise can find ways to minimise and hold down the cost of gaps between output and sales. Efforts can also be made to balance this cost with the risk of dissatisfied customers who cannot obtain sufficiently prompt delivery or service. The pressure on a business to synchronise production and sales is increasing through the growth of e-commerce. The flows of communication from the customer down each line in the supply chain are being converted from a slow manual format into an instantaneous electronic network that brings demand and supply into much closer contact. In future it will be even more important to make sure that production and sales work together.

What type of premises?

There are always appropriate premises for a business. Finding them in the right location can be time consuming and frustrating. In selecting the right premises businesses would normally consider the following:

- personal circumstances of the owner – whether to work part- or full-time, flexible hours, alone or with colleagues, and whether to employ staff or not have to be decided
- location, e.g. access, parking, whether the business relies on passing trade or has a regular customer base
- finance, e.g. set-up costs, rent, overheads, who has responsibility for repairs and decoration, insurance costs, business rates, etc
- legal issues, e.g. restrictive covenants attached to the deeds, the lease or the tenancy agreement, planning permission and change of use, local bye-laws, licence requirements, other legal requirements and restrictions
- security and safety concerns
- equipment, facilities, space, comfort and ambience
- if an existing business is being purchased then the reputation of the established business, volume of its work, size of client base, profitability, etc need to be taken into account.

These general considerations can all be forgotten if there is an overwhelming case for special exceptions. Little Dippers is an example of a business which had to forget all the rules.

> **The choice of premises is influenced by:**
>
> - **appearance**
> - **cost**
> - **size**
> - **layout**
> - **physical environment.**

 ASE STUDY

Little Dippers 4

Having decided to set up her water safety business, Lauren needed to have the right premises for training. Not all local swimming pools are usable. Each pool had to be checked and approved as young babies need a hydrotherapy swimming pool with warm water. The lack of appropriate swimming pools has been a major barrier to further business expansion.

Figure 6.21 In hot water (Reproduced by permission of Zena Holloway)

In selecting the right business premises, the owner can work from a number of different types of location. These include the following.

Working from home
Many self-employed people prefer to work from home. It is not just journalists and designers who do so; many forms of self-employment lend themselves to home working.

Table 6.6 Home working

Advantages	Disadvantages
• Overheads will be lower • Convenient • No travelling to work • You may not need to be near the customers	• You may need planning permission • You may disturb the neighbours • Difficult to separate family and business life

Serviced offices
There are a number of specially designed spaces for small business, provided by some local authorities, universities and business centres. These can be offices, workshops or just a shared desk but they provide

access to secretarial assistance, an answering service, photocopiers and other office equipment. These are cheap and flexible premises which often suit the needs of new businesses. In some centres, there are staff who are able to advise new businesses.

Teleworking

There are over 4 million teleworkers in the UK. They work at home, using technology and communications software to do their job. Some of the teleworkers are employed by companies but others are self-employed. This might be an attractive option for some new businesses, particularly when face-to-face communication is not important. Typical self-employed teleworkers run businesses as journalists, translators, writers, proofreaders and computer analysts. Teleworking would obviously not suit any entrepreneur whose business sells to a large number of customers.

Separate business premises

Finding the right place to set up in business can be difficult. In many situations you will need to be close to your market. The maxim that business success is based on 'location, location, location' is often well deserved.

There are various people and organisations who will help new businesses find suitable premises if the owner decides not to work from home:

- people involved in similar businesses to the one you are interested in; they may be prepared to offer you the benefit of their experience and save you a lot of time and expense
- the local Business Link, Enterprise Agency, Chamber of Commerce, local Federation of Businesses or Industries and local authority Economic Development Unit can offer information and advice on choosing premises
- high street banks and building societies produce small-business packs and have small-business advisers to provide information on the choices available
- books and guides on self-employment, especially if they are specific to your profession, are useful sources
- local estate agents and business transfer agents can provide details on the location and availability of premises
- the planning department of the local authority provides advice on planning laws, restrictions, conservation area requirements, and planning permission
- solicitors and accountants will provide the legal and financial advice on suitable premises.

What plant, machinery and equipment do we need?

Plant, machinery and equipment are all forms of fixed capital or fixed assets – tangible things that facilitate production and remain in the firm for a fairly long period of time. Every business – whether trading through manufacturing or services – needs some fixed assets of this kind.

The importance of quality

The nature of customer demand varies but quality is almost always important. Productive capacity must be matched with the degree of quality that the business intends to assure. Generally, higher levels of quality will require more sophisticated equipment with more skilled and committed staff.

How will quality be assured?

Customers expect a product to fulfil the claims made by the seller and to meet their reasonable expectations. Failures in quality during the production process are wasteful and time consuming to correct. But failures in quality that reach the market not only create dissatisfied customers but also damage the firm's reputation. Quality is as important for services as it is for manufacturing. Apart from administrative errors, failures in service quality tend to emerge at the stage of delivery to the customer. This is especially serious when the product largely consists of service quality.

Some small firms maintain a system of quality control where both the production process and end products are checked for conformity with the specification set. However, it is often less costly and more effective to ensure that quality is an in-built feature of everything that the business does. This will mean that:

- everyone understands the need for quality and the ways in which quality is to be achieved
- individuals and teams take responsibility for quality in their own work
- the business develops a culture of quality where substandard performance is not acceptable to anyone.

This approach is called Total Quality Management (TQM). It has been formally adopted by many large firms, but in a small business it is often the example set by the owner or manager that matters most. Quality is often more a state of mind than a measured outcome.

As a business grows, a more formal accreditation of quality may be needed. The British Standards Institute (BSI) offers the internationally recognised ISO 9000 certification of quality throughout the firm. This involves demonstrating a comprehensive range of quality management systems and procedures followed by checks on compliance. Although this carries a significant cost, it is likely to be more than offset by a reduction in waste, gains in efficiency and by enhanced value and reputation in the market.

When purchasing and installing plant, machinery and equipment, there are several key factors to consider:

- the reliability of the assets for the processes planned and the likely quantity of output
- the initial cost of the assets and their eventual value when taken out of use
- the efficiency of the assets in operation including their likely maintenance costs
- the maximum capacity that should be available
- the flexibility of the assets in meeting different levels and types of production
- the level of technology to be adopted and the skills required in its use.

Resolving these factors into a business decision will depend on analysis of the target market.

Note!

The US quality expert, Philip Crosby, says: 'Quality has to be caused, not controlled.'

Key term

Total Quality Management means striving to achieve high standards of quality in every activity performed by the organisation. It involves every employee and embraces their dealings with one another as well as with customers.

Figure 6.22 *Up to standard (Reproduced by permission of the British Standards Institute)*

Kaizen can be successful because employees, working in teams under the supervision of a team leader, are given the responsibility and authority to design their own jobs. Working collectively each team will discover ways to improve the operation of the business, increase the quality of the product or service and improve their own working conditions. This belief in teams, who are multi-skilled, recognises the value of employees to the business and motivates staff.

BS EN ISO 9000

The British Standards Institute (BSI) was set up in 1901 to develop National Standards in the UK to help businesses become more efficient and competitive. The main quality assurance standard of the BSI is the BS EN ISO 9000, which provides a framework for managers to ensure quality is continually reviewed. For a business to register with the BSI it would need to:

- say what the business will do
- write this procedure in a quality manual
- do what the business says it will do
- make sure the system is effective
- make improvements to the system.

To maintain the award of the BSI standard the business has to ensure its quality system works and continues to work effectively in practice.

Kaizen

Another approach to maintaining the quality of the business's products or service is Kaizen. This Japanese technique emphasises the importance of small, gradual improvements and allows the business to continually improve its performance and remove inefficiencies.

Finding the right suppliers

Finding businesses to supply you with the necessary raw materials can be time consuming. People who are new to self-employment may not have the necessary contacts and may not know whether they are getting a good price and high quality service for their important supplies. There are various organisations which will provide assistance and help, such as:

- trade publications, professional journals and the classified columns of special interest magazines
- self-employment guides and standard texts in the chosen profession
- business fact sheets on the particular profession, available from high street banks and building societies
- other professionals and people engaged in similar businesses
- local Business Links, Enterprise Agencies, Chambers of Commerce, professional and trade associations
- trade directories available in the public library
- telephone directories such as Yellow Pages and Thompson's.

Taking advantage of these sources will prevent a new business from getting stuck with an unreliable or expensive supplier.

After you have found a reliable supplier, at the right price, it makes sense to build up a long-term business partnership. Over time each business will come to depend on the other. This should ensure each business responds to the other's needs. In some areas these business relationships are very strong and the purchasing business is able to introduce changes within the supplier's business. One area where a strong relationship is required concerns the timing of deliveries of raw materials or components. Whenever a purchasing business is pushed for time it is important to be able to rely on its suppliers. If they are not able to deliver on time, then the purchasing business will not be able to meet its own production and supply commitment. This problem can arise even with simple things like the supply of headed notepaper or a working photocopier.

Who are the best suppliers?

Traditionally, British businesses have encouraged suppliers to compete against each other to get the work. Managers have often insisted upon three quotes, in writing, before anything can be ordered. Even when the business has needed to re-order, the supplier which won the initial order will often need to re-tender in case someone else is cheaper. This competitive system is rapidly being replaced by new relationships based upon trust. This new philosophy is built upon four premises:

- Supply will be for a long time. This will enable the suppliers to plan for the future and improve their own production techniques through capital investment.
- Supply benefits both parties. Both the supplier and the manufacturer benefit from having well established contracts. The supplier is able to reduce the risk of being in business and the manufacturer makes savings in the costs of production.
- Fewer suppliers are needed. It is much easier to work with a few suppliers, thereby creating better working relationships.
- Better-quality suppliers are needed. Businesses will only survive with good quality products and control over quality begins with the raw materials and components.

These changing relationships have taken a long time to happen and most businesses now recognise that suppliers are very important in ensuring the quality of their own products. To build up the necessary trust and commitment takes a long time. Not many businesses have the resources to deal effectively with a wide range of suppliers, so being able to work closely with a few suppliers is very important. In selecting which suppliers to choose there are five basic considerations:

- the quality of the product or service
- the location of the supplier
- the technical competence and reliability of the supplier
- the price of the goods or services supplied
- the supplier's willingness to work co-operatively.

Once the business is happy with the suppliers there are potential financial savings and reductions in waste.

Business to business trade

One area where the Internet is producing savings for companies is in business to business (B2B) trade. The volume of trade is growing and is expected to be worth $805 billion in America by 2003. Hundreds of trade sites exist on the Internet, allowing potential customers to seek the best prices while maintaining high quality and reliable service.

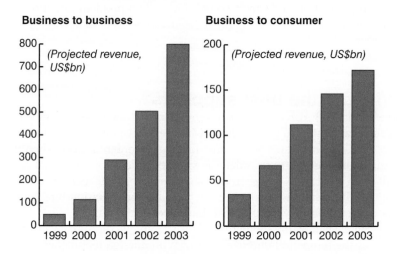

Figure 6.23 The shape of e-sales to come (Source: Dataquest)

Want to know more?

Many businesses aim to reduce the time taken from receiving an order to the delivery of a finished product. This is achieved by using the concept of Just in Time. In manufacturing industries this works by providing the parts and materials only when they are needed by the next stage in manufacturing. This applies to the component suppliers as well as each stage in the production process in the factory. By ensuring delivery of components and parts just before they are needed the company can hold lower stocks of spare parts and thereby save money. This system also allows a business to become more flexible and respond to any changes in consumer demand.

Key term

Just in Time is an arrangement whereby manufacturers ensure that their raw materials and components are delivered by the suppliers only when they are needed.

Investigating your suppliers

In the same way that you may wish to check that someone you sell to has the ability to pay, suppliers may also wish to investigate your

business. Many organisations will provide credit for small purchases such as the cost of an advertisement in a local paper. If your business places small orders on a regular basis or places an order for an expensive item, you might be asked for any of the following:
- permission to approach the bank to check your finances
- your latest set of accounts
- a trade reference from another supplier.

Your supplier could also approach a credit reference agency to see if any information is held on your business.

What are the stages of production?

A production process is usually made up of many activities and needs careful planning. The aim is to ensure that customer demand can be met promptly without holding wasteful levels of stock. The most basic supply chain includes the activities shown in Figure 6.24.

This is more complex to manage than it first appears to be. Usually there are a number of suppliers whose products are needed at different stages in the overall process. Then there may be a range of distributors (e.g. a number of retailers) who will order different products in different quantities at different times. Within the production process itself, there are usually a number of distinct stages.

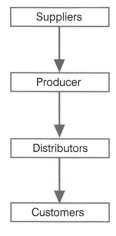

Figure 6.24 Basic supply chain

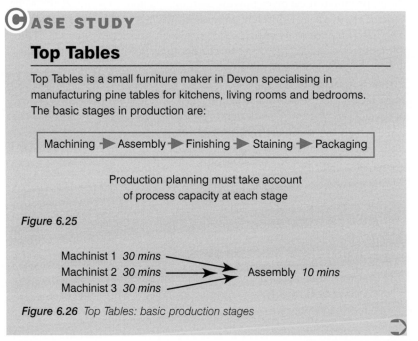

CASE STUDY

Top Tables

Top Tables is a small furniture maker in Devon specialising in manufacturing pine tables for kitchens, living rooms and bedrooms. The basic stages in production are:

Machining ➤ Assembly ➤ Finishing ➤ Staining ➤ Packaging

Production planning must take account of process capacity at each stage

Figure 6.25

Machinist 1 *30 mins*
Machinist 2 *30 mins* ➤ Assembly *10 mins*
Machinist 3 *30 mins*

Figure 6.26 Top Tables: basic production stages

Top Tables has three machinists each taking about 30 minutes for their work. One assembly worker taking 10 minutes per table can then cope with the flow of six tables every hour.

In practice there is often a risk of bottlenecks as speeds of output in successive stages move out of alignment. Suppose that at Top Tables some timber that is partly ready-cut arrives. Now the machinists take only 20 minutes on each product. The result is that nine sets of table components reach the assembly process every hour. This is a 50 per cent increase in workload and a backlog will quickly build up. Either one of the machinists needs to be taken out of the chain or some extra capacity at the assembly stage is needed.

What are the main types of production?

Job production

Job production treats each item of output as a unique and separate project. The firm's resources are used in a unique combination to meet the needs of one customer. Special materials may be ordered and craft or professional skills put to a one-off use. Machinery and equipment may be specially set and individually applied. Job production is expensive but may add a high level of customer value.

Batch production

Batch production involves making a group or batch of items at the same time. If there are any differences between the items they are very minor. The batch moves in its entirety between each production process. This allows more efficient use of resources but does not offer much flexibility.

Flow production

Flow production requires a stream or flow of resources through a series of specialised and purpose-designed processes. Initial overhead costs are usually high but these are then spread across a large volume of output. Bulk ordering of materials and other inputs combined with less skilled labour also helps to keep costs down.

CASE STUDY

Three cake companies

Creative Cakes is a small business offering a bespoke service. Individual cakes are made to order in accordance with customer requirements. Relative costs and prices tend to be high.

Country Cakes is a medium-sized firm where batches of cakes are made to the firm's own recipes. All the cakes in each batch move through successive production stages together. Relative costs and prices are moderate.

Catering Cakes is a large firm where a limited range of cakes for the catering industry is produced in a continuous flow. Individual cakes move along a production line that starts with basic ingredients and ends with boxed cakes. Relative costs and prices are low.

The difference between these production formats is tending to become blurred through the impact of new technology. Machines are becoming more flexible in being able to carry out a range of tasks at high speed and low cost. Machinery resetting times are falling. Even machines themselves are getting less expensive relative to the tasks that they can perform. The result is that the costs of job and batch production are often falling. Meanwhile flow production is getting more adaptable and able to offer customised options. 'Mass customisation' means the use of flow production technologies that allow an output of different products.

In business terms this all means that firms can take their product range closer to the real needs of customers. Not only can a market segment be better served but it may be possible to identify and satisfy micro-segments that would once (not long ago) have been too small for profitable targeting.

> **Key term**
>
> **Mass customisation** is the large-scale production of goods or services that are differentiated in the process to meet different customer requirements.

 Market segment, page 3

How should production be timed?

As a business plan unfolds in practice, it is likely that flows of work for different customers will be needed at different times. This makes production scheduling important. For example, some processes may be heavily used and a 'slot' for a particular order will need to be 'booked' – consistent with delivery to the customer on time. Coded charts are often used to plan and monitor production. For more complex operations they will be on computer.

Table 6.7 Simple production planning chart

Week	10	11	12	13	14	etc
Process A	Brown's		Black's	White's		
Process B	Pink's	Green's	Brown's	Black's	White's	
Process C		Pink's	Green's	Brown's		
		Delivery date for Pink	Delivery date for Green	Delivery date for Brown		

In the above table there is no flexibility in fulfilling Green's order, which must be ready for despatch at the end of Week 12. Brown's order needs a week in Process A but this could be Week 10 or Week 11. However, it is vital that Brown's order undergoes Process B in Week 12 and Process C in Week 13. Notice that slack does occur in Processes A and C while Process B is fully booked. Any missed production times here may make deliveries late.

Using a computer for the business

An important aspect of an operations plan is how, and whether, the business will make use of computers. Many small businesses use computers to help plan their work, not just in the production of invoices, letters and advertising copy. The computer brings order to the work of a busy office, provided there is sufficient expertise to take advantage of its power. The main advantages of a computer for a small business are as follows:

- It encourages and fosters efficient and routine operating practices.
- It can be a vital planning tool in the pre-start-up phase to see if a business is viable – spreadsheets can be used to forecast financial needs, the levels of sales needed to reach break-even point and targets that the business needs to meet if it is to make a profit.
- Word processing software and a good printer provide a quick and simple route to creating a professional and consistent image for the business. Mistake-free and professional documentation such as letters, price lists, invoices, regular orders, brochures, leaflets, advertisements, etc can be standardised and run off when necessary.
- The ability to store large amounts of information and text for later use saves a considerable amount of time and prevents unnecessary duplication of effort. It also provides the flexibility of extracting information held in different files and combining text, tables, spreadsheets and graphics to create new documents.
- It can be used to improve the marketing of the business. Databases can be created of customers' names and addresses, spending records, etc, which can then be used to analyse what is being sold in what quantities to whom, what services are being used, how often and by whom. Personalised letters can be created and sent as direct mail (or e-mail or fax) to existing customers or potential customers obtained from commercial mailing lists.
- It can be used to monitor stock, alerting the business if items are required and assisting the owner to reduce the amount of stock held (and hence, the amount of money tied up in stock).
- Spreadsheets and specialist packages enable even very small businesses to record, monitor and analyse management information on the performance of the business which would be time consuming and expensive to do manually, e.g. sales figures, income, cash flow, etc.

 Breaking even, page 49

Figure 6.27 *Is it really needed?*

Do you need a computer?

Although there are many advantages of using a computer for a small business, it may not always be a good idea to spend money in this way. For some businesses these advantages are just not large enough and the effort involved outweighs the benefits. Some of the main problems facing small businesses with computers are as follows:

- Computers can consume vast amounts of staff time which might otherwise be spent on more productive aspects of the business.
- Mistakes in selecting the most appropriate hardware, peripherals (monitor, printer, scanner, modem) and software can be costly. A great deal of time, research and specialist advice is necessary before the final purchase is made.
- Because of the value of the equipment and the information stored on it, there is always the risk of theft. Additional funds will be necessary to ensure adequate security measures for the premises and to prevent unauthorised access. Accidental damage is also a possibility and can lead to the loss of vast amounts of vital information. Insurance against fire, theft and accidental damage is an essential expense.
- It is also necessary to ensure that all information held on the computer's hard drive is regularly backed up onto disc or a zip drive and, if necessary, onto paper so that in the event of power cuts, theft or mechanical failure, all client and business details are not lost.

Financial plan

Start-up balance sheet

Once the business has been set up, the owner can prepare the initial balance sheet. This will show the assets, capital and liabilities before the business starts trading.

Balance sheet as at 1/1/2001

Assets		£	£
Fixed assets			
Premises			21,000
Current assets			
Stock		2,000	
Cash		500	
Bank		3,000	
		5,500	
Total assets			26,500
Liabilities			
Short-term loans			
Amount owed and to be paid within one year	(1,500)		
Working capital			4,000
Total assets less current liabilities			25,000
Long-term loans			
Amounts to be paid after more than one year			10,000
Capital			
Initial investment			15,000
			25,000

> the difference between current assets and current liabilities

Figure 6.28 *Opening balance sheet*

In the above example, the business was set up with £26,500. This has been used to buy appropriate premises (£21,000), stock for trading purposes (£2,000) and the remainder of the investment is held as cash or is in the bank account. The business has been financed from the owner's own funds (£15,000), a mortgage secured against the premises (£10,000) and from trade creditors (£1,500).

ACTIVITY

How much of the £26,500 investment has come from external sources?

Preparing the starting balance sheet allows the business to make comparisons in one year's time besides demonstrating an understanding of the business finances. The starting balance sheet, a cash flow forecast and break-even analysis are required by lenders who wish to see the business's potential.

Will the cash flow?

All businesses occasionally experience problems with collecting money owed to them. This is a real problem for new businesses as all the expenses have been incurred but the invoice has not been paid. Despite legislation, since 1998, allowing for interest payments for late payments of commercial debts, many small businesses feel unable to charge because it damages their relationships with clients. There are various ways of reducing the risk of non-payment of moneys owed:

- ask for part of the money to be paid at the time of the order
- take out insurance in case of non-payment
- use a shared bank account where the purchaser puts money in and the supplier takes it out
- arrange special payment terms
- give a cash discount
- give a rebate for prompt payment
- ask for a guarantee from a third party
- keep the legal ownership of the goods until payment is made
- use a credit collection agency to recover debts.

These measures can help a business ensure that it is paid and on time. Another more general approach is to work closely with customers and build up close business relationships so that each becomes reliant on one another. When a business has only a few customers this approach can be very effective, though it would not work for all business, e.g. those in the retail industry.

Businesses often allocate a risk code to each of their customers:

- **A – no risk because of good payment record**
- **B – average risk since occasionally there is a late payment**
- **C – high risk because they are late payers and may not be able to pay.**

Sometimes, when there are not enough A and B customers, businesses have to work with customers with a high risk rating.

The cash flow forecast

Even when all the creditors pay the full amount on time, there will be different amounts of cash coming into the business each month. Businesses can help themselves by predicting their own flow of incoming and outgoing cash. This cash flow forecast allows the business to estimate its financial position and when it may need to borrow money. In the example from Three 2 Four Ltd from 2000, the business expected to

Table 6.8 Cash flow forecast for Three 2 Four 2000

	January	February	March	April
Opening cash balance	10,000	11,560	12,870	12,160
Cash sales	3,500	3,400	3,500	
Credit sales	2,000	1,000	2,200	
Total income	**15,500**	**15,960**	**18,570**	
Wages	1,200	1,200	1,200	
Purchases	2,480	1,520	1,560	
Telephone		250		
Electricity			450	
Other costs	260	120	3,200	
Total expenditure	**3,940**	**3,090**	**6,410**	
Balance at the end of the month	11,560	12,870	12,160	

have a very healthy cash balance (see Table 6.8). This money could be used more productively than leaving it in the business.

ACTIVITY

How could Three 2 Four make better use of the £10,000 extra cash that appears to be unused in its business?

Some businesses know that there will be a seasonal imbalance in their income and need to plan for these variations. Businesses that are based on tourism, agriculture, Christmas shopping, etc can all predict when the busy season will arrive. This may result in the business having to borrow money for six months of the year during which time the stock levels are increased to meet the seasonal demand. Once the income starts, the business will be able to pay off its loans and make a profit. These businesses run the risk that the expected upsurge in demand during the buying season will not happen.

In addition to the need to control their profits, businesses have to be concerned about their cash flow as liquidity is a very important factor for success. As a general rule all businesses attempt to improve their cash flow by:

- keeping a close eye on all cash payments
- working hard to collect all money that is owed
- slowing down the payment of their own bills.

In these ways as much cash as possible is kept within the business, thereby allowing more flexibility and less need to borrow money.

The product life cycle

With the launch of any new business, the financial situation is affected by the product life cycle. The diagram below shows the different stages of the product life cycle and the corresponding effects on the business's cash flow.

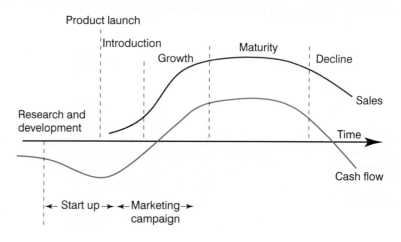

Figure 6.29 *Product life cycle and cash flow*

Will the business break even?

Besides the cash flow forecast and the starting balance sheet, new businesses should prepare a break-even analysis. Not only is this required by lenders, it also helps the entrepreneur understand the costs and revenues for the business. It also allows for businesses to plan what would happen if something changed.

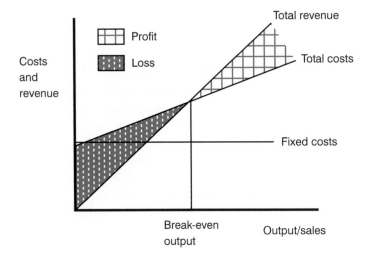

Figure 6.30 Will it break even?

The diagram outlines the number of items that have to be sold before the business starts to make a profit. It also indicates the consequences of not selling enough – the business will make a loss.

ACTIVITY

Little Dippers 5

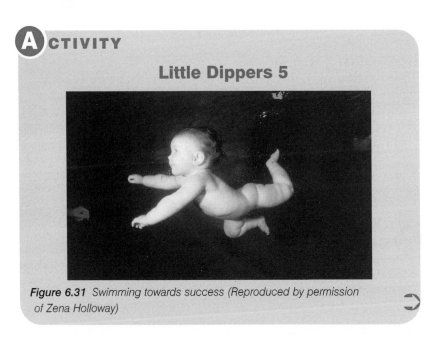

Figure 6.31 Swimming towards success (Reproduced by permission of Zena Holloway)

Lauren Heston's Little Dippers Club runs different courses at different levels and the babies can progress from the introductory to the advanced course. The costs of each course can be separately identified, allowing Lauren to establish how many clients are needed to ensure she makes a profit on each course. The maximum number of babies on each course is eight and because of the demand nearly every course is full. The cost for the hire of a swimming pool for one hour is £23. This is enough time for one of the 30-minute training sessions. The costs for each training session are:

	£
The trainer's wages	15
Contribution to office expenses	10

Each parent pays £40 for a set of five training sessions for their baby. How many customers does Lauren need on each training course before she makes a profit? If the course is full, how much profit is made?

Will the business make a profit?

Forecasting helps the new business plan for the future. The profit and loss account, the cash flow and the break-even chart can be predicted, though this is no guarantee that profits will be made. Businesses can also make use of spreadsheets to work out what happens if sales rise, prices fall or costs increase. This 'what if' technique allows some degree of experimenting with the financial success of the business. Any forecast or testing of the finances is only as good as the information used. The belief of 'garbage in, garbage out' is just as relevant to finance as it is to computing.

Improving the profit

There are many ways to improve the profitability of a business. Each approach needs to be tried if profits are falling or lower than expected. Three of the options are to:
- cut costs
- increase prices
- increase sales.

Whilst it is easy to increase prices quickly, cutting costs or increasing sales takes longer.

 **A**CTIVITY

Complete the following table, to identify the advantages and disadvantages of each of the above three approaches to increasing profit.

Table 6.9 Increasing profit

	Advantages			Disadvantages		
	1	2	3	1	2	3
Cut costs						
Increase price						
Increase sales						

How do you measure success?

Success in business is usually thought of in terms of financial success. This is one measure but it is not the only way of deciding success. Many people set up in business because they want to work for themselves or because they want to develop their own ideas. To measure how successful they have been you need to know the objectives they have set themselves.

Mission statement, page 19

Financial success

 **ASE STUDY**

J and P Builders

John and Paulo started working together in 1989 and set up their own business two years later. They work as semi-skilled builders, prepared to do most areas of labouring and skilled work. They started their business with £1,000 of their own and a £4,000 loan from the bank. The business has been quite successful and each year they have seen their incomes gradually rise. They know they will not be millionaires but they earn enough to support their families, even though they work long hours. In the past seven years the business has shown the following improvement.

Table 6.10 Financial success

	1994	1995	1996	1997	1998	1999	2000
Turnover	41,880	46,360	65,360	78,500	79,060	73,000	78,000
Drawings (income)	20,650	22,980	30,820	34,890	35,600	35,400	36,930

One measure of success would be to consider the rise in their personal income. Another way would be to look at turnover. These are rough indicators to give a general idea of business performance but for a fuller picture John and Paulo would need to use ratio analysis.

John and Paulo's business can be evaluated by using the standard ratios that cover:
- the business's profitability
- the business's liquidity
- the return on capital employed (ROCE).

Even if the owners of the business are not interested in financial success, their bank manager will be. The bank would examine the accounts if John and Paulo tried to expand their business and wanted to borrow more money. Their business appears to be successful and they have few problems in meeting the monthly interest repayments on their loan.

Do the finances work?

There are many ways of looking at the financial success of a business. Ratio analysis is the main approach but businesses can also look at long-term trends, their own success compared to that of their competitors, whether they meet their own targets or whether the current venture is as profitable as investing in another business. All of these approaches are valuable to established businesses, but they are not very useful for a new organisation. Without the necessary data and information newly establishing businesses cannot work out whether they are a success.

An alternative way for new businesses to consider whether the finances work, or will work, is to answer some questions such as:
- Is the percentage profit on the investment greater than what could be earned in a bank?
- Does the business allow the owner to maintain the lifestyle wanted?

- Does the future look good?
- Does the cash flow work?
- Is running the business too much of a risk?
- Is running the business too stressful?

Profit and loss account
for the year ended 30/4/01

	£
Sales revenue	78,000
Cost of sales	(12,400)
Gross profit	65,600
Overheads	23,800
Net profit	41,800

Balance sheet of J and P Builders
as at 30/4/01

Assets	£	£
Fixed assets		
Office		4,240
Van		4,350
Current assets		
Debtors	1,580	
Cash	120	
Bank account	3,470	
	5,170	
Total assets		13,760
Liabilities		
Current liabilities		
Trade creditors	(1,280)	
Working capital		3,890
Total assets less current liabilities		**9,870**
Long-term liabilities		
Bank loan		4,000
Capital		
Opening capital		1,000
Net profit for the year	41,800	
Less drawings		(36,930)
		9,870

Figure 6.32 Is this success?

On page 11 we looked at whether you were suited to running your own business. At the end of the book it is appropriate to reconsider these questions. Despite the possible financial success, for some people the risks are too great. The hassle and stress can be overwhelming and the amount of work involved may not be commensurate with the rewards. These are decisions that can only be made by the individual and it is wrong to assume everyone is able and prepared to be self-employed.

Plans and reality

New businesses can make grand plans. Sometimes these are realistic but not always. Variance analysis is a valuable way of assessing the success of a business and planning the future. Variance analysis considers the difference between the planned finances and what actually happened. This allows the owner of the business to identify the problems and work out some solutions.

CASE STUDY

J and P Builders 2

The turnover of John and Paulo's business has continued to rise – £78,000 in 2000. This was their best year but it was not as they had planned. In 1999, with turnover at £73,000, their forecast was an increase in turnover to £90,000. This forecast was based on three assumptions:
- they had an increasing loyal customer base
- the economy was expanding and business was booming
- increasing their prices would not affect the number of customers.

An analysis of 2000 showed what happened.

Table 6.11 J and P builders' budgets

	1999	Planned 2000	Actual 2000	Variance
Number of customers	80	90	78	12
Average price	£912.50	£1,000	£1,000	–
Turnover	£73,000	£90,000	£78,000	£12,000

Variance analysis can identify what went wrong. The difference between the planned and actual financial performance can be caused by a difference in price, a difference in quantity or a combination of both. In the case of J and P Builders the problem was caused solely by a fall in the number of customers.

**CTIVITY**

What could have caused the problem?
What solutions would you recommend for J and P?
What extra information would assist your analysis?

Other types of success

In addition to evaluating the financial success of a business, many commentators look at other ways of assessing success. Two frequently used approaches are environmental audit and social audit. Each takes a wider view of the business and considers its contribution to society. Environmental auditing is widely accepted amongst large organisations. Social auditing started in the mid 1990s with well known companies such as Ben and Jerry's (now owned by Unilever plc) and the Body Shop but has not been accepted by all companies.

> ### Key terms
>
> **Social auditing** is a way of measuring the social and ethical performance of an organisation.
> **Environmental auditing** is a way of measuring the environmental contribution of an organisation.

**ASE STUDY**

United Biscuits

'Some employees might have the mistaken idea that we do not care how results are obtained as long as we get results. This would be wrong. We *do* care how we get results. We expect compliance with our standards of integrity throughout the company, and we will support an employee who passes up an opportunity or advantage which can only be secured at the sacrifice of principle. Beliefs and values must always come before policies, practices and goals. The latter must be altered if they violate fundamental beliefs.'

This extract from the ethics booklet from United Biscuits, issued in 1987, shows how some businesses recognise the importance of standards in business. This is one company's attempt to resolve the conflict of interest between stakeholders by setting a standard of behaviour for all its employees.

ASE STUDY

Whole Earth

In 1995, Whole Earth was awarded the award of Best Organic Foods Range for its products. The family-owned business, launched in 1967, is proud of its ability to:

- support environmental and fair trade charities
- apply the highest ethical standards when dealing with co-workers, suppliers and customers
- strictly control all ingredients to exclude genetically modified or irradiated materials
- trade with over 2,000 organic farmers across the world.

And it aims to make a profit! The business does not only measure its success by the profit it makes but by its performance against the ethical, social and environmental aims in its mission statement.

Figure 6.33 *High standards*

The two examples above illustrate the importance of other indicators of success. It is not only financial returns that matter. With businesses increasingly recognising the importance of all the stakeholders in business, other factors have to be considered before the organisations can be regarded as successful.

Want to know more?

Measuring the performance of a business or predicting its future success is difficult without objective evidence. The best way to predict is to use indicators showing how value is created. These will indicate the business's long-term success and its competitiveness. The three main indicators of value creation are:
- marketing performance, e.g. growth of sales, customer satisfaction, brand names
- operational performance, e.g. productivity, quality control
- innovation, e.g new products, skills of the staff.

Based on *The Guardian*, 18 September 1999

Want to know more?

There are a number of new ways of measuring success. These have been created because the standard accounting ratios provide financial information and do not always give the full picture of how well the business is doing.

Economic Added Value: The difference between a company's post-tax operating profit and the cost of the capital invested in the business. This is sometimes called 'economic profit'.
Market Value Added: The difference between a company's market value and the total capital invested – this is the wealth created by the stock market.
Cashflow Return on Investment: This compares the inflation-adjusted cash flows with inflation-adjusted gross investments to find cash-flow return on investment.
Total Shareholder Return: What the shareholder actually gets, i.e. changes in the capital value of shares plus the dividends on these shares.

Based on *The Observer*, 12 January 1997

What are the milestones?

As a business grows and develops, the owners need to be able to establish key points in the business's success or failure. This allows owners to recognise whether they have met their own aims besides providing a warning if things are not going as planned. Establishing milestones allows an early warning system to operate. Some milestones may be very short-term indicators such as: what percentage of the sales is going to existing customers; whether sales are continuing to rise; or whether your existing customers recommend you to new clients. Longer-term milestones may well involve opening another office or branch of the business, employing an assistant within twelve months or reaching a turnover of £100,000 after two years. It is helpful to establish indicators of success (and failure) at the start of the business so that corrective measures can be taken if necessary.

The business life cycle

Businesses progress and expand at their own pace – some thrive early in their development while others collapse quite quickly. Successful businesses have a life cycle of their own. If they continue to trade they pass through five distinct stages:

The start-up stage

This is usually the owner controlled business which is run to provide income for the family and to provide self-employment.

Expansion

This occurs when new markets are being sought. To successfully reach this stage, businesses often need more finance.

Consolidation

The business becomes more entrepreneurial and some risks are taken. There is usually considerable expansion in the business's existing markets.

Development

The business begins to consider takeovers and mergers in addition to continuing its expansion in all existing markets. This is usually a time of raising additional funds from external sources.

Maturity

The business has become as large as the current owners would like. Once the mature stage has been reached, the business may not stop growing. Although the current owners may be satisfied with the size of the business, other owners (either new shareholders or businesses) may see further growth potential.

The future

CASE STUDY

Little Dippers 6

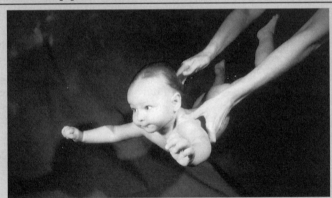

Figure 6.34 Entering the deep end (Reproduced by permission of Zena Holloway)

Now that Lauren Heston's Little Dippers Club is successful, there are a number of ways she could branch out. Before any of this could happen Lauren wisely registered Little Dippers as a trade mark. While the business was small this was not necessary, but without protection another organisation could take advantage of her success. The first new business outlet to be created was a casting agency which works with film crews and the mothers and babies. Other ideas currently being considered are:

- using mother and baby photographs for postcards
- using mother and baby photographs for birthday cards and congratulations cards
- product endorsements, particularly clothes for babies
- further work with film crews.

The potential for great photographs makes these ideas a real possibility. An example of this diversification occurred in May 1998 when a photograph of a Little Dippers' customer was used on the front page of the *Radio Times*.

 Trade marks, page 27

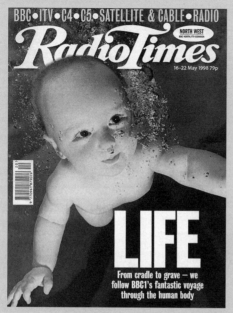

Figure 6.35 The start of further success (Zena Holloway/Radio Times 16–22 May 1998, reproduced with permission)

Little Dippers has reached the expansion stage of its business life cycle (see page 57) and is almost at the consolidation stage. Deciding what to do at this point in a business's development is difficult. Many entrepreneurs decide that the problems of further expansion are too much to handle. Others branch out into related activities. This gives a more diverse portfolio of business activities and reduces the risks of being self-employed.

CASE STUDY

homepro.com

New businesses are being set up every day. Some succeed but many fail. The increased availability of the Internet has provided additional opportunities for new businesses. Many of these Internet based businesses offer a new way of buying a product or service, rather than something completely different; for example, book selling via Amazon.com, music via MP3 technology or simply buying from existing retailers through their website.

Figure 6.36 *Avoiding cowboy builders*

 Sources of external finance, page 13

A recent addition to the range of dotcom organisations is homepro.com, formerly called hirevolution. Its origins are based on an American business, improvenet.com, and it aims to match local contractors with householders looking for help with decorating, building and design. This is not a new idea: Yellow Pages offers a similar service, as do national trade associations. As with most Internet based businesses homepro.com offers something extra. The company, set up with nearly £1,000,000 of venture capital, provides a vetting service to ensure contractors' work is of high quality and, in response to a request from a householder for names of approved contractors, homepro.com considers where people live, the contractor's availability for work, the householder's budget, etc. The company provides four approved contractors with the householder's telephone number and asks each to offer a quote to complete the work. The householder is free to select from one of these quotes or not. This matchmaking service allows householders to employ contractors with confidence.

As Kim Rehfeld and Adam Burdess, homepro.com's directors, are keen to point out: 'Cowboy builders have created enormous problems of trust in home improvements, and thousands of quality professionals have been tarred with the same brush. Homeowners and good contractors are fed up with the situation. By pooling their collective experience of home improvement and allying with the professionals dedicated to quality, homeowners now have the opportunity to run the cowboys out of town. At homepro.com, we aim to make the process of making your home a better place to live much more fun, cheaper, quicker and less stressful.'

The business aims to sell to customers in well-paid jobs. The company has identified its market segment as those customers in socio-economic groups ABC1, aged between 20 and 40. Their advertising is mainly through the Internet. Before the company was launched nationally, homepro.com carried out direct marketing via a mailshot in Kent to test the idea behind the business. Since its establishment, homepro.com has also advertised in regional newspapers. The company is aiming for 500,000 customers once the business is well established.

 Market segments, page 3

CTIVITY

Tasks

1 How does homepro.com offer added value?
2 Homepro.com has to market its services to two groups: builders and customers. What approaches would you advise for each of these groups?
3 The company, although different in size from a small local business, faces similar problems establishing itself. What are the main challenges the business is likely to face in its first year of operation?

Appendix: Key Legislation

Copyright, Designs and Patents Act (1988)
This Act gives protection to the inventor, designer or originator of an idea.

Consumer Protection Act (1987)
The Act makes provision for customers to take legal action against a supplier for injury caused by a defective product whether the product was sold to them or not and without having to prove the supplier was negligent. The Act also covers misleading price indications about goods, services or facilities available from a business.

COSHH – Control of Substances Hazardous to Health Regulations (1988)
The regulations require employers to identify hazardous substances in the workplace and control people's exposure to them (e.g. by careful handling, storage, and labelling, prompt clearance of spillage and provision of adequate ventilation).

Data Protection Acts (1984, 1998)
These Acts cover businesses, the self-employed and homeworkers who keep information, no matter how little, on computer about any living person. Almost any information other than a name, address and telephone number (with a few other exceptions) places an obligation to register with the Data Protection Registrar. Individuals have the right to see any computerised information held on them and to have incorrect information amended or deleted.

Once a business is registered, a Code of Practice is issued which requires the business to: keep the information secure; ensure the information is accurate and relevant to its needs; comply with individuals' right to see any computerised information held on them and to have incorrect information amended or deleted.

Disability Discrimination Act (1995)
This gives people with disabilities new rights in three main areas: employment; access to goods, facilities and services; the management, buying or renting of property.

Discrimination occurs when, for a reason related to his or her disability, a person is treated less favourably than other people and this treatment cannot be justified. The Act also set up the National Disability Council to advise government on discrimination against people with disabilities.

Electricity at Work Regulations (1989)
These regulations cover general safety in the use of electricity which includes the operation and maintenance of electrical equipment in a business. They provide for

- regular checking of equipment by a competent person (not necessarily an electrician)
- listing of checks in a record book stating results, recommendations and action taken in the case of defects, and signature of the competent checker

Employers Liability (Compulsory Insurance) Act (1969)

This Act places a duty on employers to take out and maintain approved insurance policies with authorised insurers against liability for bodily injury or disease sustained by employees in the course of their employment.

Employment Protection (Consolidation) Act (1978)

This Act sets out the framework for employees to obtain compensation or reinstatement through an Industrial Tribunal if they have been unfairly dismissed. This gives employees the right:

- not to join a trade union on religious grounds
- to join a trade union
- not to be unfairly selected for redundancy
- to be able to return to work following maternity leave
- not to be dismissed for strike action if other employees who also went on strike have not been sacked.

Equal Pay Acts (1970, 1984)

The 1970 Equal Pay Act was introduced to end discrimination between men and women, in basic rates of pay and other terms of their contract of employment (e.g. overtime rates, bonus agreements, holiday entitlements, etc). This was amended in 1984, as a result of European Community legislation, to enable men and women to claim equal wages for work of equal value done for the same employer or an associated employer. Any employee can claim equal pay if the work done is:

- of 'like work' to that of a colleague of the opposite sex
- equally rated under a proper job evaluation study
- of equal value in terms of the demands made.

EU Council Directive (90/270) (1993)

The directive lays down minimum safety and health requirements for the users of computer screens or visual display units (VDU). Employers (including home workers) are expected to evaluate the risk to themselves and their staff from computer equipment, software and the working environment.

Factories Act (1961)

This places an obligation on an employer to provide a safe place of work.

Fire Precautions Act (1971) (updated in 1976)

The Act requires a business to provide fire-fighting equipment in good working order, readily available and suitable for the types of fire likely to occur. The Act also specifies that room contents should not obstruct exits, so that a quick escape, in the event of fire, is not impeded.

Gas Safety (Installation and Use) Regulations (1984)
This relates to the use and maintenance of gas appliances used in a business. British Gas and Health and Safety Executive inspectors have the right to enter premises and disconnect dangerous appliances under the Right of Entry Regulations (1983).

Health and Safety (First Aid) Regulations (1981)
The regulations require that all businesses must have an appropriate level of first aid treatment available in the workplace. This means that businesses must:
- appoint a person to take charge in an emergency and look after first aid equipment. There must be an 'appointed person' available at all times during working hours
- provide and maintain a First Aid box containing information/guidance on the treatment of injured people regarding:
  - how to control bleeding
  - how to give artificial respiration
  - how to deal with unconsciousness
- display notices which state:
  - locations of first aid equipment
  - name of person(s) responsible for First Aid.

Health and Safety at Work Act (1974) (updated by Workplace Health and Safety Welfare Regulations 1992 (EC Directives))
Employers should ensure the provision of adequate toilet and washing facilities, machines that are electrically safe, and protective clothing or equipment; they must ensure that precautions are taken when using chemicals; they must provide and a clean and tidy workplace for their workforce. The self-employed, home workers and people who work alone away from employer's premises are included.

Employers are required to:
- provide systems of work that are, so far as is reasonably practicable, safe and without risk to health.

Employees have responsibility to:
- take reasonable care of themselves and other people affected by their work
- co-operate with their employers in the discharge of their legal obligations.

Human Rights Act (1998)
This came into effect in October 2000 and covers everything a public authority (local government, national government, government agency, etc) does. It provides a basis for the protection of the fundamental rights of every citizen. All public authorities have an obligation to ensure that respect for human rights is at the core of their day-to-day work.

Questions that public authorities need to ask include:
- Is a person's ability to carry out a trade or profession affected?
- Is a person's physical or mental well-being affected?
- Is a person's private or family life affected?
- Is any individual or group being discriminated against, on any basis?

If the answer to these types of question is yes, an individual may be able to bring legal action against the public authority.

Offices, Shops and Railway Premises Act (1963)

The Act stipulates minimum standards to ensure safe and healthy working environments. In conjunction with the Health and Safety at Work Act, it relates to every part of a business's premises.

Businesses should also make provision for a clean, tidy, well lit, well ventilated and well maintained workplace, a clean and tidy workforce, adequate toilet and washing facilities, machines that are electrically safe, protective clothing or equipment, control of noise and vibration, accident and fire prevention, the safe use of chemicals and dangerous substances, safe transportation and safe handling of materials.

Race Relations Act (1976)

This Act defines three types of discrimination, all of which are illegal:
- direct discrimination on racial grounds that treats a person less favourably than others are or would be treated in the same circumstances
- indirect discrimination that applies a requirement or condition which, whether intentionally or not, adversely affects a particular racial group considerably more than others
- discrimination by means of victimisation that treats a person less favourably than others because that person has made a complaint or allegation of discrimination.

The Act also established the Commission for Racial Equality which has direct responsibility for monitoring the effect of the Act.

Reporting of Injuries, Diseases and Dangerous Occurrences Regulations (1985)

These regulations cover occupational disease, serious injury or death in connection with a business. A report must be sent to the local authority if:
- there is death or serious injury in an accident at work
- anyone is off work for more than three days as result of an accident at work
- specified occupational disease is certified by a doctor.

Employers are required to record in an accident book any accident or case of disease required to be reported (preferably signed by all parties concerned).

Sale of Goods Act (1979)

Associated with the Supply of Goods and Services Act 1982, the Unfair Contract Terms Act 1977, the Supply of Goods (Implied Terms) Act 1973 and various EU directives.

The Act covers consumer rights when purchasing goods from a business. Goods must be as described, of merchantable quality and fit for their intended purpose. The Act also covers the conditions under which the customer can return goods.

Sex Discrimination Acts (1975, 1986)

These Acts declare that it is unlawful to be treated less favourably because of one's sex or marital status. Discrimination can be considered under two headings:

- direct discrimination occurs if a person is treated less favourably than a person of the opposite sex is (or would be) treated in similar circumstances
- indirect discrimination occurs when a person is unable to comply with a requirement, which on the face of it seems to apply equally to both sexes, but which in practice can be met only by a much smaller proportion of one sex.

Social Chapter (1997)

The Maastricht Summit in December 1991 adopted the 'Social Chapter' within the European Union. The UK accepted this in 1997. Some of the main sections of the Social Chapter are as follows:

- freedom of movement within Europe
- the right of all EU nationals to receive equal treatment to that received by nationals of the host nation
- all employment is to be 'fairly remunerated'
- the establishment of controls on the organisation and flexibility of working time, including a maximum working week
- protection for employees engaged in other than full-time jobs of indefinite duration (part-timers, temporary workers, shift-workers, etc)
- the right to annual leave and a weekly rest period
- every EC citizen to have 'adequate social protection'
- the right to a 'minimum income' for all workers excluded from the labour market without being able to claim unemployment benefit
- the right of employees to belong to any professional organisation or trade union
- the freedom to negotiate and conclude collective agreements
- the right to take collective action, e.g. to strike
- equal treatment between men and women
- further developments to ensure satisfactory health and safety conditions at work, including a movement to standardise in the European Union
- a minimum age of employment of 16
- the right of young workers to vocational training for at least two years.

Sunday Trading Act (1994)

If the floor area of the sales area is less than 280 square metres there are no restrictions on opening hours on Sunday, otherwise retailers can only open for six hours.

Supply of Goods and Services Act (1982)
This extends the protection for consumers provided by the Sale of Goods Act 1979 to services. The person or business providing the service must do so:
- for a reasonable charge
- within a reasonable time
- with reasonable care and skill.

Trade Descriptions Acts (1968, 1972)
These Acts prohibit the use of false descriptions of goods and services provided by a business. For any retailer the provisions apply where the description is given by another person (such as the manufacturer) and then repeated to the client or customer.

Trade Union and Labour Relations (Consolidation) Act (1992)
The Act provides protection for employees who are dismissed for being members of trade unions.

Trade Union Reform and Employment Rights Act (1993)
This entitles every employee who works for more than 16 hours a week to receive an itemised pay slip at or before each payment of salary.

Transfer of Undertakings Regulations (1981)
These regulations provide employees with protection when their business is taken over by new employers. Prior to the regulations (usually referred to as TUPE), an employee's existing conditions and terms of employment would not be transferred to a new employer. All employees were considered as having no statutory rights associated with continuity of employment. This was changed with the European Union's Acquired Rights Directive in 1997 which provided:
- that employment contracts are automatically transferred from one employer to another
- protection from dismissal as a result of, or for reasons related to, the transfer
- that employers are obliged to inform and consult with employees' representatives before the transfer.

Unfair Contracts Terms Act (1977)
This prevents anyone from including an unreasonable clause in a contract.

Wages Act (1986)
This Act restricts the employer's right to take money from the employee's wages unless the deduction is:
- a legal requirement
- part of the employee's contract and the employee has been notified in writing
- agreed to by the employee in writing.

Index